0.98

24.26

SEAS AND OCEANS

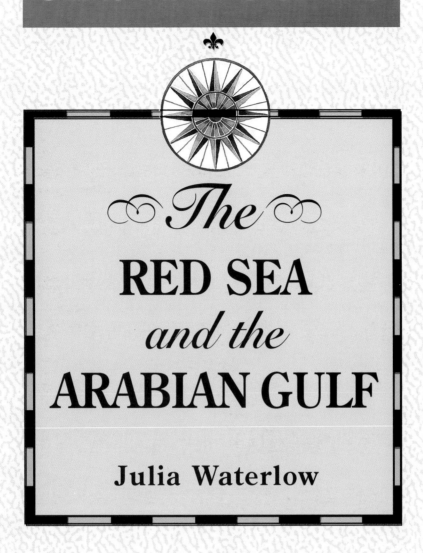

The
RED SEA
and the
ARABIAN GULF

Julia Waterlow

RSVP

RAINTREE
STECK-VAUGHN
PUBLISHERS
The Steck-Vaughn Company

Austin, Texas

Seas and Oceans series

The Atlantic Ocean
The Caribbean and the Gulf of Mexico
The Indian Ocean
The Mediterranean Sea
The North Sea and the Baltic Sea
The Pacific Ocean
The Polar Seas
The Red Sea and the Arabian Gulf

Cover: A coral reef in the Red Sea

© **Copyright 1997, text, Steck-Vaughn Company**

Published by Raintree Steck-Vaughn Publishers,
an imprint of Steck-Vaughn Company

Library of Congress Cataloging-in-Publication Data
Waterlow, Julia.
The Red Sea and the Arabian Gulf / Julia Waterlow.
    p.   cm.—(Seas and oceans)
    Includes bibliographical references (p.) and index.
    Summary: Examines various aspects of the Red Sea and Arabian, or Persian, Gulf and the lands around them, discussing their physical features, weather, sea life, human inhabitants, and natural resources.
    ISBN 0-8172-4515-4
    1. Red Sea—Juvenile literature.
    2. Persian Gulf—Juvenile literature.
    [1. Red Sea. 2. Persian Gulf.]
    I. Title. II. Series: Seas and oceans (Austin, TX)
GC741.W38 1997
551.46'733—dc20   96-40997

Printed in Italy. Bound in the United States.
1 2 3 4 5 6 7 8 9 0 01 00 99 98 97

Picture acknowledgments:
Dieter Betz 12, 15, 27 (bottom), 36, 45; James Davis Travel Photography 9, 14, 16, 29 (right), 33 (top); Ecoscene 18, (Mark Caney), 20 (top right/Mark Caney), 34 (Adrian Morgan); Eye Ubiquitous 5 (Christopher Portway), 13 (Paul Dowd), 20 (bottom left), 37 (Paul Dowd), 40 (Paul Dowd), 41 (Julia Waterlow); Impact 28–9 (top/Alan Keohane), 38 (John Norman), 39 (Caroline Penn), 44 (top right/ Schurr/ Cedri); Frank Lane Picture Agency 19 (Ian Cartwright), 21 (Ian Cartwright), 24 (R. Commer/Earthviews), 25 (E&D Hosking), 41 (A. Parker); Oxford Scientific Films 23 (David Fleetham); Panos Pictures 31 (Guy Mansfield), 32 (Alain le Garsmeur); Planet Earth Pictures 22 (Georgette Douwma); Science Photo Library 11 (NASA); Tony Stone Worldwide 26 (Nabeel Turner), 27 (top), 42 (Chris Haigh), 43 (Jeff Rotman), 44 (bottom left); Julia Waterlow 7, 28 (bottom), 30; Zefa *cover* (Tekano).
All artwork is produced by Hardlines except Peter Bull 33 (bottom).

Contents

Words that appear in **bold** in the text can be found in the glossary on page 46.

INTRODUCTION
The Desert Seas

The Red Sea and Arabian Gulf are like a finger and thumb of water, pointing up from the vast Indian Ocean into the part of the world known as the Middle East. To the east is the **continent** of Asia; to the west, Africa; and to the north, Europe. The Red Sea and Arabian Gulf lie on the crossroads between these continents.

The two seas are almost entirely surrounded by land, but they have narrow channels at the southern end joining them with the Indian Ocean. Between the seas is a block of land known as the Arabian **Peninsula**. The shimmering greens and blues of the water contrast with the sun-scorched yellows and browns of the coasts, since much of the land around is barren desert.

The Red Sea and the Arabian Gulf lie in the Middle East. The Arabian Gulf is also sometimes known as the Persian Gulf and is often shortened to "the Gulf."

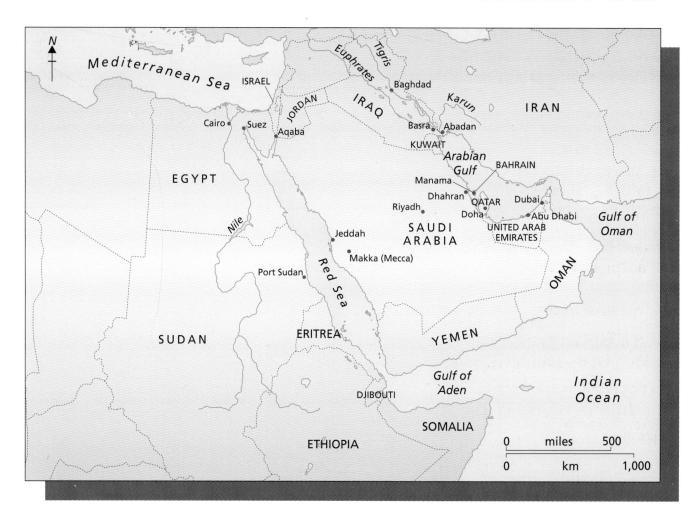

The deserts and lack of water mean that the land is sparsely populated. Saudi Arabia, for example, has an area ten times that of Great Britain, yet its population is only a quarter of the size. There are only a few settlements on the Red Sea coasts, but in the Arabian Gulf there are new ports and modern cities that were built when oil was discovered in the area. Not long ago, the people of the Arabian Gulf lived simple **subsistence** lives. Now the countries around the Arabian Gulf are among the world's richest, because oil has brought great wealth to this area. In contrast, neighboring countries that do not have oil are much poorer.

The Red Sea and Arabian Gulf are relatively small compared with the great oceans. Even so, they are important seas. The Arabian Gulf has the largest **oil reserves** in the world, and fleets of oil **tankers** sail across its waters. Although the Red Sea has not been developed in the same way as the Arabian Gulf, it is a vital international waterway linking the Mediterranean Sea with the Indian Ocean via the Suez Canal. The Red Sea also has a very special natural feature—some of the longest and most unspoiled coral reefs in world.

At Abu Dhabi, on the Arabian Gulf, a crew takes a boat to go fishing in the shallow waters along the sandy desert coasts.

The Red Sea

The Red Sea is long and thin, running almost north to south. It separates the shores of Africa and Arabia—on the west side lie Egypt, Sudan, and Ethiopia and on the east side lie Saudi Arabia and Yemen.

In the far north, the Red Sea divides into two narrow stretches of water: the Gulf of Suez and the Gulf of Aqaba, split by the Sinai Peninsula. A small neck of land divides the Gulf of Suez from the Mediterranean Sea, but the Suez Canal has been cut through the **isthmus** so that ships can travel from one sea to the other. The Red Sea narrows at its southern end, and a **strait**, called the Bab al Mandab Strait, connects the Red Sea with the Gulf of Aden.

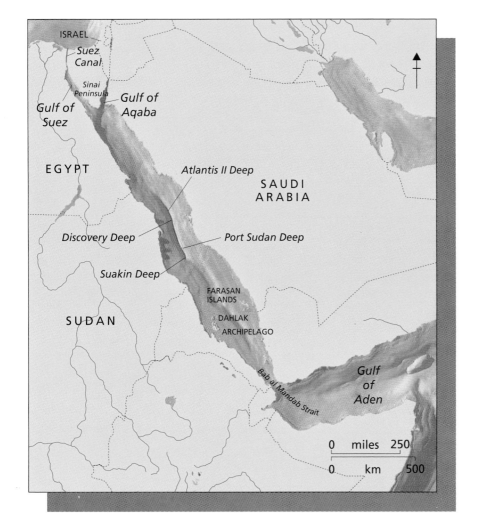

The Red Sea is like a long, thin trench filled with water. Although shallow around the edges, the Red Sea plunges deep down in the middle.

The size of the Red Sea
Area: 169,000 sq. mi.
Length: 1,200 mi.
Maximum width: 190 mi.
Maximum depth: 9,600 ft.

Although the Red Sea is shallow near the coasts, it drops down to great depths in the middle. Running along the center of the Red Sea is a deep trough, or underwater valley, which in places is very rugged. Here, several sharp clefts, like deep pits, appear in the seabed and plunge 9,600 feet below sea level.

Among the special features of the Red Sea are its coral reefs. The reefs occur mostly near the coasts in shallower waters and stretch for thousands of miles around the edges of the sea. In places, the coral has grown across harbors, such as at Suakin in Sudan. In the southern part of the Red Sea, the coral growth has left only narrow channels that ships can sail through, and at the Bab al Mandab Strait the coral has to be blasted and **dredged** so that ships can pass through. Over the centuries, many ships have been wrecked on the Red Sea coral reefs, and treasure hunters still find ships that sank more than 2,000 years ago.

There are islands dotted around the Red Sea, but they are nearly all uninhabited. Many are exposed coral reefs with just sand or a few bushes, but near the Dahlak Archipelago there is a group of active volcanoes.

This tourist village lies on the coast of the mountainous Sinai Peninsula, which divides the Gulf of Aqaba from the Gulf of Suez at the northern end of the Red Sea.

The Arabian Gulf

The Arabian Gulf is about half the size of the Red Sea and is shorter and wider. Like the Red Sea, the Gulf is **landlocked** at its northern end, and a narrow channel, called the Strait of Hormuz, joins it to the Gulf of Oman and the Indian Ocean. Lying to the west is the Arabian Peninsula, and to the east lies Iran.

The Arabian Gulf is a very shallow sea; in places it is no deeper than 300 ft. The seabed slopes gently down from west to east, with the deepest water along the coast of Iran where the rugged Zagros Mountains come down to the sea. The Arabian coast is low-lying and fringed by sandy beaches, mud flats, and **lagoons**. Sandy islands, such as Bahrain, lie offshore. Around the narrow Strait of Hormuz, cliffs plunge into the sea, and the rocky coast and small islands make it a dangerous area for shipping.

On the Arabian side, the Gulf is shallow with sandy islands and lagoons; on the Iranian side, the water is deeper and the coast is much rockier.

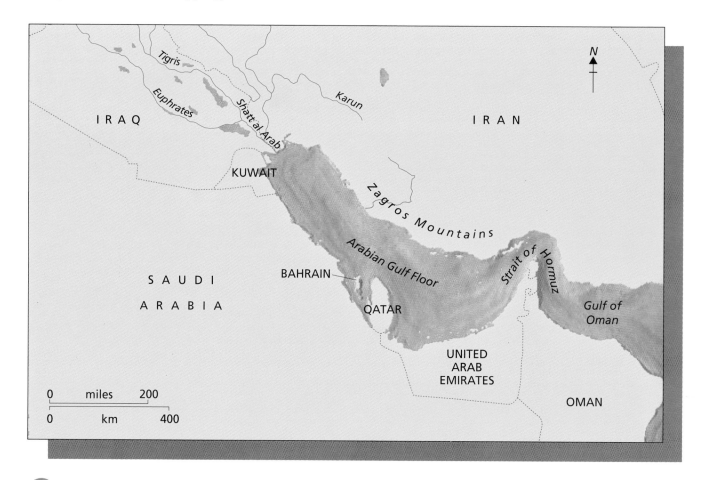

The size of the Arabian Gulf	
Area:	93,000 sq. mi.
Length:	615 mi.
Width:	Between 210 and 220 mi. at Hormuz
Depth:	Mostly no more than 300 ft.

At the northern end of the Gulf, there is a wide plain where three rivers, the Tigris, Euphrates, and Karun, flow out into the sea. Over thousands of years these rivers have brought huge amounts of **sediment** downstream. The sediment has been dropped as the rivers slowed down and reached the sea and created a low-lying marshy **delta**.

The Arabian Gulf may once have been part of a much larger, deeper basin, which has gradually been filled by sediment. Some sediment would have been blown from the land or carried down by rivers, and some would be the remains of dead sea creatures. The thick layers of sediment (hundreds of feet deep) have left the surface of the sea floor very smooth. Oil and gas have formed in these sediments.

Much of the Gulf has shallow, clear water such as here off the coast of Abu Dhabi.

The Moving Earth

The Red Sea lies in a gap between Africa and Arabia, where the earth is being pulled apart. The surface of the earth is made up of pieces of hard crust, known as plates. These float like skin on molten rock that lies deep in the earth, where it is very hot. Driven by the heat below, the plates slowly move around, sometimes colliding with each other and sometimes splitting apart. They usually move at a rate of a few inches a year.

Geologists think that Africa and Arabia started moving away from each other about 30 million years ago, although the most northern and southern parts of the Red Sea may have only opened up about 4 million years ago. The trough that appeared filled with seawater from the Indian Ocean.

The crust of the earth is broken up into plates that slowly move around, splitting apart and colliding. This map shows what is happening in the Middle East and in East Africa.

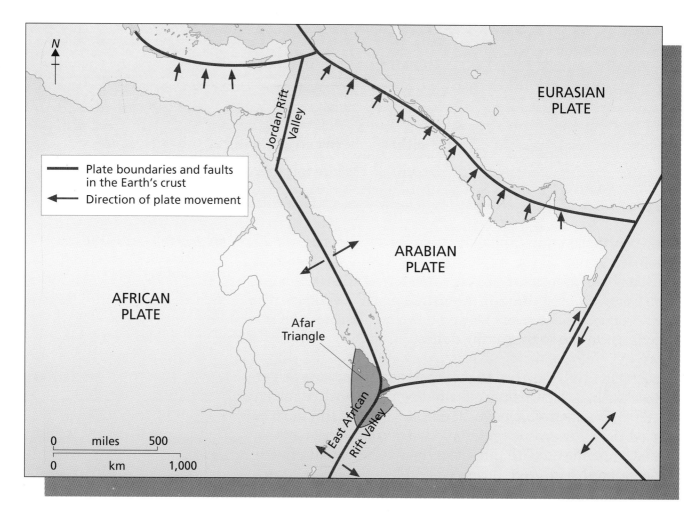

Part of the Afar Triangle in Djibouti as seen from a satellite. The inlet of water at the bottom right is part of the Gulf of Aden. The red landscape is mostly bleak and desolate rock. The black patches are lava (molten volcanic rock) flows, and the white areas are salt lakes.

The Red Sea is a relatively new sea in terms of the **geological history** of the earth, and it is growing. If the African and Arabian plates continue to spread apart at their present rate, in 200 million years the Red Sea will become as wide as the Atlantic Ocean.

The trough filled by the waters of the Red Sea is part of a long system of cracks in the earth's crust caused by the stresses and strains of plate movements in this region. The East African Rift Valley continues south for about another 2,200 mi., and the Dead Sea–Jordan Rift Valley is a trough that carries on north from the Gulf of Aqaba.

The Afar Triangle

The Afar Triangle is a flat triangle of land on the African side of the Red Sea. It lies at the very southern end of the Red Sea, where it meets the Gulf of Aden and the East African Rift Valley and is part of the trough caused by the spreading continents.

The Afar Triangle was once covered by the sea, but earth movements lifted the land above sea level. It is an area of inhospitable desert covered in thick layers of salt left by the sea and with the remains of old volcanoes.

In contrast to the Red Sea, the Arabian Gulf lies where two plates of the earth's crust are colliding. As the Red Sea has split apart, the Arabian plate has been pushed eastward and collided with the much larger Eurasian plate. The Arabian plate has buckled and been pushed downward at its eastern edge along the coast of Iran. This is why the seabed slopes down to the east and the water is deeper there. Pressure on the Eurasian plate has caused it to crumple and created the mountains behind the Iranian coast.

Cloudless Skies

The Red Sea and Arabian Gulf lie in one of the hottest, driest parts of the world. Daytime temperatures in summer can be more than 104°F and in winter are rarely less than 68°F. The north is usually a little cooler than the south: Winter temperatures in Kuwait have been known to fall as low as 37°F.

What little rain there is usually falls as short, heavy showers in the winter months of January and February. In the Gulf state of Bahrain, for example, it only rains ten days a year on average, and the total rainfall in most of the area is under 4 inches a year. Tropical storms are rare, although in winter there are sometimes sudden **squalls**, which cause waves big enough to sink small ships.

A stiff breeze blowing across the Red Sea. Although this helps local fishermen with their sailing boats, it can also make the water quite choppy.

A sandstorm in the deserts of the Arabian Peninsula. Winds can bring dust and sand swirling down to the sea.

Most of the land around the two seas is desert, which reaches down to the edge of the seas. There are no lakes and few rivers. The only rivers in the area are the Tigris, Euphrates, and Karun, and the Nile River, which lies east of the Red Sea and flows north into the Mediterranean Sea.

The climate is hot and sticky, mainly because of the very high humidity caused by the sea and the high temperatures. There are few clouds to keep the sun off, and the air feels sticky and stifling at times. The intense heat causes a shimmering haze over the water and land, making it difficult to see very far.

Both the Red Sea and the Gulf have persistent **seasonal** winds, although they are rarely strong enough to cause very dangerous seas. The winds often bring clouds of sand and dust from the deserts, sometimes completely blotting out the sun. Winds in the Red Sea are mostly northerly, but during winter, strong westerlies blow up (called the Egyptian winds), bringing fog as well as sand.
The most common wind in the Gulf is the shamal, which blows from the north mainly during summer.

Desert rivers

The Tigris and Euphrates rivers, which flow through the deserts of Iraq, are fed by rain and melted snow in mountains to the far north. The river valleys provide fertile and well-watered land for farming in an area with extremely low rainfall. Before reaching the Gulf, the rivers wind through lakes and marshes and finally join to become one channel, called the Shatt al Arab, which flows out into the sea. The rivers used to flood in spring and bring tons of sediment down to the Arabian Gulf, but now river flow is controlled by dams. More than 90 percent of the rivers' water never reaches the Gulf—it either **evaporates** in the hot sun or is drawn off and used for watering crops.

Salty Seas

Salinity (Parts per thousand)	
Red Sea	
Average salinity	36
Gulf of Suez	40
Deep clefts	257
Arabian Gulf	
Average salinity	40
Arabian coast	60

Both the Red Sea and Arabian Gulf are very salty seas. The amount of salt in seawater is referred to as salinity and is measured in parts per thousand. The average seawater salinity in the world is about 35 parts of salt to every 1,000 parts of water. Both the Red Sea and the Gulf have considerably higher salinities.

Most seas are filled by fresh water from rivers, which makes them less salty. But very little fresh water enters either the Red Sea or Arabian Gulf. Also, the hot sun causes huge amounts of seawater to evaporate (more than 78 in. a year). Salt does not evaporate with the water but remains in the sea, so the water that is left becomes even saltier. The Gulf's salinity is higher than that of the Red Sea because it is shallower.

Coastal salt flats (called sebkhas), along the Gulf coast in the United Arab Emirates. The Red Sea and the Arabian Gulf are some of the saltiest seas in the world.

The narrow straits at the southern end of the seas mean that they are only slowly refilled by water from the Indian Ocean. If they were completely landlocked and not refilled by ocean water, they could dry out completely. It is thought that there have been times in the past when the Bab al Mandab Strait was blocked, and the waters of the Red Sea evaporated, leaving a broad, salt-covered valley.

Dry deserts, such as this one in Egypt, surround the Red Sea on both sides. There are no permanent rivers to bring fresh water into the sea.

Surface water in both seas is very warm, but deeper, the water is much cooler. Deeper water is also saltier, because salty water is heavier than fresh water, so it tends to sink. The deep clefts of the Red Sea have a peculiar feature. These clefts have pools of hot and very salty water, with temperatures as high as 212°F and salinity five times higher than on the surface. Because the clefts lie in the middle of the sea, where the continental plates are pulling apart, it is thought that the heat and salt come from molten rock pushing up where the earth's crust is thin.

Surface Temperatures	
Red Sea	up to 89°F
Deep clefts	140 to 212°F
Arabian Gulf	over 91°F

Currents and Tides

Currents are strong movements of water in the sea that flow in one direction, rather like rivers. Surface currents in the Red Sea and Arabian Gulf are driven by winds that, in general, push water south during summer and north in winter. These currents are quite weak, except where the land narrows, such as at the Strait of Hormuz. Here, tidal water rushes through and, with the shifting and uncertain winds that blow around the cliffs, makes it a difficult and dangerous passage of water to **navigate**.

Arab traders, such as these sailors in Dubai, have used the currents and winds of the Gulf for hundreds of years to sail these waters and reach far beyond.

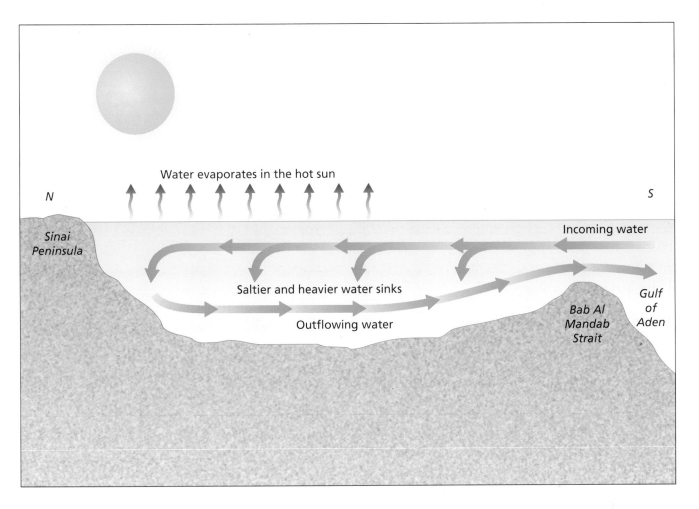

The strongest pattern of water circulation in the region is vertical, from the surface down to the depths. In the Red Sea, for example, water enters the region from the Indian Ocean through the Bab al Mandab Strait. As it warms up, the water begins to evaporate. It becomes saltier and heavier and starts to sink. This heavier water flows south underneath the incoming water from the ocean. It is thought that it takes 20 years for the water in the Red Sea to be completely renewed. Water circulates in the Gulf in a similar way.

Tides are caused by the gravitational pull of the moon. The waters of the Red Sea and the Arabian Gulf rise and fall every day because tidal water from the Indian Ocean sweeps in and out through the narrow straits at the southern end of both seas. The **tidal range** is small, at most about 6.5 ft., and the effects of the tides are seen only at northern and southern ends of the seas. Rather like water sloshed from one end of a bath to the other, water in the middle tends to stay fairly level, while at the ends it rises and falls. At Port Sudan on the Red Sea, for example, there is hardly any tidal effect at all.

One of the features of both the Red Sea and the Arabian Gulf is the way the water circulates vertically. Water entering the Red Sea from the Indian Ocean is driven northward by winds. A lot of water evaporates, especially in the shallower parts of the sea such as the Gulf of Suez. This leaves saltier water, which sinks and flows out under the lighter, incoming water.

SEA LIFE
Coral Reefs

Divers come from all over the world to explore the beautiful coral reefs set in the clear waters of the Red Sea. The reefs are like underwater walls and terraces, covered in colorful and strange-shaped corals and teeming with fish and other sea creatures.

Coral is made up of hundreds of tiny living creatures, called coral polyps, which are joined together. Coral polyps are related to sea anemones: They are tube-shaped with a mouth at one end that is surrounded by tentacles. They feed off tiny animals that drift past.

The reef's variety

Coral comes in all sorts of shapes and colors, depending on water temperature, waves, and the amount of light. Delicate branched, fan-shaped, and soft corals grow in sheltered waters; hard, rounded "brain" corals grow on the outside edge of the reef, where there are waves that would damage other kinds of coral; platelike corals spread out in deeper waters to make a large surface area to catch as much light as possible. The Red Sea has more than 350 different types of coral.

A delicate fan coral spreads out from a reef in the Red Sea.

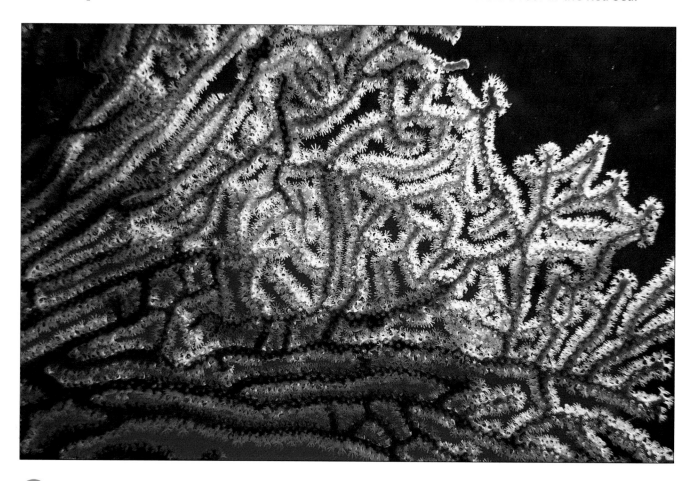

The coral reef drops down like a wall on the side facing the open sea. Colorful corals cluster on the side of the reef.

As the polyps grow, they make a hard, protective shell around their bodies that is cemented to other polyp shells. In this way, the reef builds up. The hard skeletons of dead corals make up most of the reef, but the surface is alive. Coral grows very slowly; it can take twenty years for a piece of coral to reach the size of a football. Coral will carry on growing outward and upward, but never above the surface of the water, because the polyps cannot live in air.

Coral is very delicate and needs special conditions in order to grow. Coral likes warm water, preferably where the temperature is between 71 and 82°F. Since reef-building coral needs sunlight to help it grow, it only lives in shallow water, usually no deeper than 100 ft. For the same reason, coral needs clear water, without sediment or pollution, so it does not tend to thrive where rivers carry mud and **silt** down to the sea. There are fewer coral reefs in the Gulf, partly because of the warmer water and also because of sediments brought down by the Tigris and Euphrates rivers.

Fringing reefs lie parallel to the shores of the Red Sea and around some of the islands, and **barrier reefs** are found farther out at sea in slightly deeper waters. Inside the fringing reefs are shallow lagoons, but on the seaward side the reefs slope steeply down.

SEA LIFE
Life on the Coral

Coral reefs are like tropical forests compared with the barren deserts surrounding the Red Sea. Thousands of different plants and creatures live there. Each living organism depends on another for food or shelter, and the reef supports a complex web of life, from tiny plants to big **predators**, such as sharks.

Some creatures attach themselves to coral and wait for food to come to them. Sea anemones have tentacles to draw in small creatures that float within their grasp, whereas sponges and giant clams filter tiny pieces of plant food out of the water. There are other animals, such as starfish, sea slugs, and sea cucumbers, that move slowly over the coral. Sea urchins are very common; they use their long, thin spines for defense and their teeth to scrape **algae** off the hard surface for food.

Schools of brilliantly colored and patterned fish swim in and out of the nooks and crevices in the coral. Many feed on algae, such as seaweed, but others, such as wrasses, eat worms, shrimps, and crabs. There are also predators, such as groupers, which eat smaller fish, and eels that use the coral

A pufferfish has blown itself up in a ball. It does this when threatened to make itself look more frightening.

The lionfish's striking markings act as a warning to predators; its deadly spines can inject poison into an attacker.

as hiding places to lie in wait for their prey. Most life is found on the outside edge of the reef, and this suits predators such as sharks, jacks, snappers, and barracudas, which patrol the open waters in search of other fish to eat.

Angelfish, butterflyfish, and damselfish are colored in bright yellows, blues, greens, and reds with stripes, patches, and spots. The colors attract other fish of the same species or warn predators that the fish is poisonous or unpleasant to eat.

Some creatures, such as the crown-of-thorns starfish and the parrot fish, eat coral. These creatures can do great damage to coral reefs. However, the greatest threat can be from people. Pollution of the sea by waste materials from houses and factories can quickly kill coral. The coral reefs of the Red Sea are relatively unspoiled because so few people live along the shores.

Butterflyfish are some of the most brilliantly colored fish of the reefs. They nearly always swim around in pairs like this.

Shallow Waters

Along the coasts of the Red Sea and Arabian Gulf are small inlets, where the water is shallow, and fine mud and sands collect. Since they are rich in organic materials, the dense muds are short of oxygen, making it difficult for organisms to survive. Even so, plants and creatures have adapted to this **habitat**.

Mangrove trees grow in some of the inlets. Their roots stick up above the level of the mud so that the trees can get oxygen from the air. These aerial roots also help support the trees when swept by waves as the tide comes in. Few trees can tolerate saltwater, but mangrove trees have a special way of getting rid of the salt through their leaves. The mangroves provide **nutrients** and shelter for many different fish and shellfish. Some shellfish, such as mussels, burrow in the mud leaving one end sticking out so that they can breathe. Crabs often burrow and wait for low tide before coming out to scavenge for food.

In the shallow waters of the Red Sea and the Gulf, there are beds of seagrass. This plant grows like a grass and provides a habitat where other plants and creatures, such as this long barbel goatfish and these wrasses, can thrive. This picture was taken in the Red Sea.

In sandy shallows, particularly along the Arabian side of the Gulf, there are large beds of seagrass. This is not a seaweed, but a true flowering plant with long green leaves and spreading roots. Seagrasses provide shelter for small sea creatures, such as fish and shrimps, which eat tiny particles of plant and animal matter that collect on and among the seagrasses.

The largest creature that lives among the seagrass beds is the slow-moving dugong. This creature grazes on seagrass. Although they can live up to 70 years, dugongs breed very slowly. Dugongs are found in other parts of the world, but because they have been overhunted and their habitat has been destroyed, the number is declining. There are about 12,000 dugongs left in the Red Sea and Arabian Gulf.

A dugong. These unusual creatures are mammals that graze on seagrass.

SEA LIFE
Other Plants and Creatures

One explanation for the name "Red" Sea is that sometimes large patches of a particular reddish-colored phytoplankton are seen drifting on the sea's surface. Phytoplankton are microscopic plants that live off nutrients in the water. They need sunlight to survive, so they float near the surface. Phytoplankton are the basis of life in the sea. Corals, fish, and other sea creatures feed on phytoplankton, and in turn these creatures provide food for others.

Since most phytoplankton are found near nutrient-rich coasts, these areas are also where the greatest number of other sea creatures are found. However, larger fish do cruise out in the

A diver swims with a whale shark. These gentle giants feed mainly off plankton.

Birds such as this sea eagle nest on islands in the Red Sea and Gulf. They survive by catching fish from the sea.

Death of the coral

Recently some large areas of coral died in the Red Sea. A thick mat of green algae had appeared, which smothered the coral and cut off its supply of food and light. A study carried out in Israel discovered that the massive growth was probably due to a volcanic eruption on the other side of the world. In 1991, Mount Pinatubo in the Philippines erupted, blasting dust into the atmosphere. The dust spread, filtered out the sun, and caused low temperatures in several parts of the world. A very cold winter in the Middle East brought cool, nutrient-rich waters up to the surface of the Red Sea. The surge in nutrients caused the sudden algae growth.

open waters of the Red Sea and the Gulf. The biggest of all are whale sharks, which are gray with white spots. Although they can grow up to 40 ft. long, whale sharks are harmless creatures and feed off tiny fish and plankton. Another large fish related to the shark is the manta ray, which can be up to 20 ft. wide. The manta ray is a flat fish with wings that flap slowly up and down as it moves through the water. Like the whale shark, the manta ray is a gentle creature and lives off plankton.

The islands and shores around the Red Sea and Arabian Gulf are so dry that little wildlife can live there. Birds such as terns, ospreys, pelicans, and sea eagles nest on some of the islands and depend on fish for their food. Some of the beaches also provide nesting grounds for turtles, such as the hawksbill, which swim to shore and dig holes in the sand to lay their eggs. When the little turtles hatch a few weeks later, they scuttle down the beach and return to the sea.

The Heart of the Muslim World

The Arabian Peninsula between the two seas is the home of the Arab people. It is also the center of the Islamic religion, whose followers are called Muslims. This religion was founded in A.D. 622 by Muhammad, and his ideas and beliefs spread throughout Arabia and the Middle East. They were carried farther afield by Arab traders into Africa and east toward India.

Today, all the countries in the Middle East are Muslim, apart from Israel. Mecca, a town in Saudi Arabia not far from the Red Sea, was where Muhammad was born and is the most holy place in Islam. Muslims from all over the world try to make a **pilgrimage** to Mecca at least once in their lives.

Thousands of Muslim pilgrims come to worship every year in Mecca, the most holy Islamic city, which lies on the Arabian Peninsula not far from the Red Sea.

As Islamic religion spread around the region, it carried with it Arabic ways of life. Therefore, as well as being Muslim, most of the countries surrounding the Red Sea and Arabian Gulf have Arabic as their language and an Arabic culture.

Iran (once called Persia) differs from the other Muslim countries of the Middle East. The people are not Arab but Persian and speak the Persian language. Long ago, there were disagreements over leadership in the Muslim world, and Islam split into two main branches: the Sunnis and the Shi'ites. Whereas the majority of the world's Muslims are Sunni, those in Iran are Shi'ite. These two branches of Islam do not always see eye to eye, and there are sometimes conflicts.

Along the southern borders of the Red Sea on the African side, the Arab races gradually give way to Africans. The peoples of southern Sudan and Ethiopia are mostly African and have their own languages. Many are Christians, not Muslims.

Above: In all but a few of the Muslim countries of the Middle East, women are expected to cover themselves from head to foot so that no parts of their bodies show.

Right: Like this man from Yemen, many of the people living along the shores of the Red Sea and Gulf are Arabic.

Arabian sheikhs

There are seven countries in the Arabian Peninsula, the largest of which is Saudi Arabia. Those countries where oil has been found are extremely rich. The Gulf states (the Arab countries fronting the Arabian Gulf) are ruled by kings called sheikhs or emirs, who are the heads of the controlling families. The royal families are very large: For example, Ibn Saud, who founded Saudi Arabia in 1932, had 44 sons by 22 wives. Today there are about 6,000 Saudi princes.

Traders and Sailors

For centuries, the Middle East was an important center of trade because it lay on the route between East and West. Arabs controlled much of the business. Many goods were brought overland by camel train, but the Arabs were also great seafarers. As long as 2,000 years ago, they traveled in their wooden ships, called *dhows*, from the shores of the Red Sea and the Gulf to India; many even reached China. Their cargoes were mainly high-priced luxuries such as spices, silks, and jewels. Arab sailors also traded in ivory, amber, iron, and slaves along the coasts of East Africa. Many set up businesses and settled in the countries they visited.

The Arab hold on trade became weaker from the 16th to 18th centuries. As their ships improved, Europeans started to sail directly to the Far East, avoiding the need for the markets of the Middle East. But when Europeans then began to **colonize** countries in the Indian Ocean, merchants used the Gulf as a trade route because it was the shortest way to take goods to and from Europe. Places such as Kuwait and Bahrain grew as staging and supply points.

Below: Once camels were used for taking goods across the deserts of the Middle East. Today these Bedouin offer camel rides to tourists who visit the Red Sea.

Above: **Dhows** *can still be seen sailing along the coasts of the Gulf.*

Pirates used to plunder ships passing through Gulf waters, and for a while the southern coast of the Gulf was known as the Pirate Coast. The British signed **treaties** in the 1800s with many of the Gulf states to control piracy and protect British supply routes to India. These Gulf states have only become completely independent of Great Britain over the last 30 years.

The Arabs were some of the first traders to sail to the Far East and bring spices to the West. Spices are still sold in markets all over the Middle East.

Overland trade through the Middle East lost its importance in 1869 when the Suez Canal was completed. By linking the Red Sea with the Mediterranean, goods could be taken directly by ship between Europe and the Far East. Nowadays, although Arab *dhows* still sail along the coasts of Africa and India, most of the seaborne trade is the endless traffic of large tankers from the Gulf, which take oil all over the world.

Slaves

For hundreds of years, one of the main seagoing cargoes on these seas was African slaves. The Arabs were some of the first to deal in the slave trade. They took Africans from East Africa for their own use and to supply European colonies in the area. At times during the 1800s, each year 10,000 slaves were being transported north to the Middle East and India. Even until the 1930s, wealthy Arab families kept African slaves to tend their livestock and to work in their households.

From Farming to Cities

As well as being great traders, the Arab people around these seas lived by fishing, growing dates, and herding animals. Because of the lack of water for growing crops, many could survive only by keeping animals that could **forage** on desert **scrub**. Some people still follow the traditional ways of life, but the discovery of oil in the Gulf has meant that most people leave farming to go to cities where there are better paying jobs.

The Bedouin are the main group of Arabian desert herders. They live in small family groups, keeping goats and sheep that graze rough grass and bushes found on the desert fringes. The Bedouin are traditionally a **nomadic** people, moving their tents from place to place in search of food for their animals.

Where there is enough water, the land is farmed. In desert **oases**, water from underground wells is used to grow wheat, vegetables, and fruit, especially dates. The most productive farming areas are the Tigris, Euphrates, and Nile river valleys, where it is also possible to grow rice, cotton, and sugarcane, crops that need more water. By using **desalinated** seawater and modern **irrigation** systems, desert is being turned into new farmland near some cities on the Gulf coast.

Right: Modern, air-conditioned buildings sprout up in the heart of Bahrain, a rich island kingdom in the Arabian Gulf.

Dates grow at the top of tall palm trees, making them hard work to harvest.

30

Lifestyles have changed most in the countries where oil was discovered. Cities and ports were built with the money from oil. People moved there to work on oil rigs, on building sites, in factories, and in offices. Today, about 90 percent of people in the Gulf live in urban areas, many of which are on the coast. Places such as Bahrain and Kuwait are very modern, with towering skyscrapers and luxurious houses with air-conditioning and swimming pools. The main industries are oil processing, supplying oil rigs, carrying out ship repairs, and cargo handling.

Foreign workers

During the 1970s and 1980s, millions of people, mostly from other Arab countries such as Egypt, Yemen, and Jordan, arrived in the Arabian Gulf to work in the oil industry. In Qatar, for example, 90 percent of the workforce is from abroad, and in Kuwait about half the population are foreigners. More recently, workers have been coming from Asian countries such as Pakistan, South Korea, and the Philippines. There are tight restrictions on where immigrants can live and work, and no foreigner is allowed to stay permanently.

There are far fewer towns on the Red Sea. Jeddah is the largest and, as well as being one of Saudi Arabia's biggest industrial ports, is the arrival point for the many thousands of Muslims who visit Mecca each year. Aqaba, Port Sudan, and Suez are important because they are the main Red Sea ports for Jordan, Sudan, and Egypt.

PEOPLE AROUND THE SEAS
Water

The key to life in this desert region is water. Where there is water, people can grow crops and build towns. In Egypt and Iraq, most people live in the large river valleys of the Nile, Tigris, and Euphrates, where there is water year-round. Israel and Jordan share water from the Jordan River. Elsewhere, villages and small towns have grown up around wells, which draw on underground reserves of water, called **aquifers**.

Over the last 50 years, the population has been growing fast and so has the need for water. In all Arab countries, the supply of water can now barely keep up with the demand. River and aquifer water is fast being used up, and in some countries water has to be piped from long distances away. It is likely that water supplies will run out before the oil, and water could become just as valuable. There are bound to be arguments over the right to use water, especially along rivers such as the Tigris and Euphrates, which run through different countries.

Building irrigation channels, such as this one in the United Arab Emirates, means that crops can be grown even in the desert.

A desalination plant in the United Arab Emirates. Here salt is removed from seawater to produce fresh water that can be used in homes, factories, and farms.

The greatest demand for water is in the growing cities of the Gulf, where there are almost no natural, freshwater supplies. As well as being used by households and industry, large amounts of water are being used for new irrigation projects to grow crops in the desert.

Seawater cannot be used because it is too salty, but it can be desalinated. This process removes salt from seawater and turns it into fresh water, but it uses a lot of fuel and is very expensive. For the oil-rich countries of the Gulf, this is no problem, and some of the first and biggest desalination plants in the world were developed there. Countries such as the United Arab Emirates, Kuwait, Qatar, and the state of Bahrain depend completely on desalination for their water.

Water from an aquifer reaches the surface in various ways.

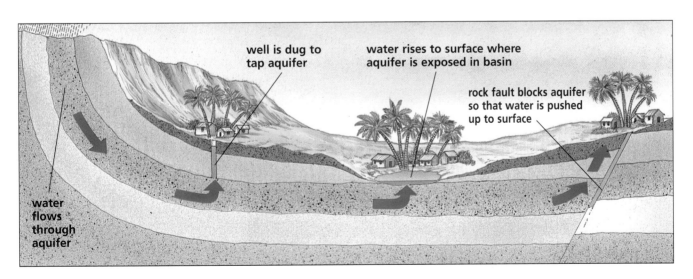

well is dug to tap aquifer

water rises to surface where aquifer is exposed in basin

rock fault blocks aquifer so that water is pushed up to surface

water flows through aquifer

THE NEW WEALTH
Oil and Gas

The Arabian Gulf is the most important oil-producing area in the world. Oil is found both onshore and offshore under the seabed. The main producers in the Middle East are Saudi Arabia, Iran, Iraq, Kuwait, and the United Arab Emirates. Between them, these countries have more than half the world's known oil reserves. They only use a small amount of the oil they produce themselves, so most of the oil is exported. The Gulf also has large reserves of natural gas.

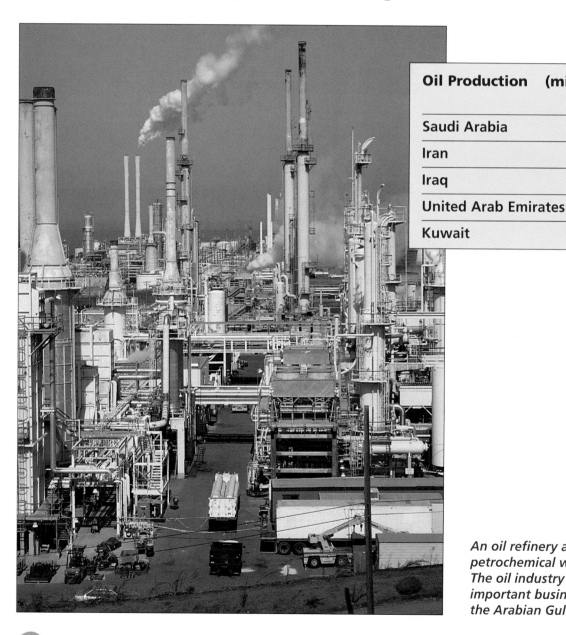

Oil Production	(million barrels per day)
Saudi Arabia	6.2
Iran	3.1
Iraq	2.1
United Arab Emirates	2.1
Kuwait	1.1

An oil refinery and petrochemical works in Dubai. The oil industry is the most important business for people of the Arabian Gulf.

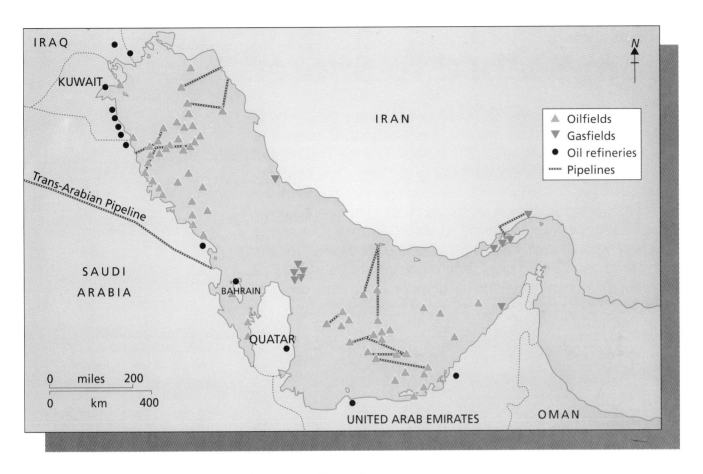

This map shows the huge number of oil fields in Gulf waters. There are also numerous oil fields and pipelines on the land and around the sea.

We could not live as we do without oil. The oil that comes straight out of the ground is called crude oil, and for most uses it has to be **refined**. It is burned as a fuel for heating houses and in power stations and is refined into gasoline and diesel fuel for cars, trucks, planes, and ships. Some oil is turned into paraffin and lubricating oil for machinery. Oil is also the raw material used to make chemicals, fertilizers, plastics, and medicines. Natural gas is used mostly as a fuel.

Oil and gas are made naturally by **organic** matter **decomposing**. Over millions of years, organic sediments that collected in the basin of the Arabian Gulf were covered by sandy and muddy sediments that hardened into rock. Through heat and pressure of the rock above, chemical changes caused the organic sediments to turn into oil and gas.

Oil and gas can filter upward through soft rock, but where they meet very hard rock they become trapped. Reservoirs of oil and gas collect under the rock; large reservoirs are known as oil fields or gas fields.

Oil Reserves	(Percentage of total world oil reserves)
Saudi Arabia	25.8
Iran	9.3
Iraq	10.0
United Arab Emirates	9.8
Kuwait	9.5

From Seabed to Shore

Expensive and highly technical equipment is needed to extract the oil from under the seabed, but the shallow and calm waters of the Gulf make it easier there than in many other seas. An oil rig consists of a metal platform, called the deck, supported on concrete or steel legs. These are drilled into the seabed to hold the rig in place. On the deck is the drilling equipment as well as living accommodations for the oil-rig workers. The rig may be far out at sea, but people work there for weeks at a time and all supplies have to be brought to them.

A helicopter brings workers to an oil rig at sea. Behind the helicopter a flare of gas burns. Gas comes out of the ground with the oil and is often just burned off.

Oil is extracted from the underground reservoir by long tubes (sometimes several miles long) that are let down through the water and drilled through the rock above the reservoir. The oil and gas are under pressure because they are squeezed by water and rocks. Once the reservoir is punctured, oil and gas pour out along the tubes to the rig above. As the reservoir empties, the pressure falls and water or gas is pumped back in to force out the oil.

Often a burning flare is seen above oil rigs, which is gas being burned off. Gas is often wasted in this way if there is just a small amount in the reservoir, because gas is not as easy to collect as oil. On gas rigs, gas is collected, converted to a liquid, and then transported in tankers, in a way similar to oil.

Oil is pumped to shore along pipes or collected by tankers and taken to storage tanks or refineries. Most Gulf oil is exported as crude oil, but Gulf states refine some themselves. Oil is shipped around the world by tanker and across the Middle East by pipelines through the desert. Two long-distance pipelines are the Trans-Arabian Pipeline, which runs from Saudi Arabia to the shores of the Mediterranean (currently unused because of political problems), and the Sumed Pipeline, which carries oil from the Red Sea to the Mediterranean region.

Pipelines such as this one in Egypt run across the deserts of the Middle East, taking oil from storage tanks by the coast to towns and cities inland. Pipelines are a relatively simple and quick way to transport oil over long distances.

USES AND RESOURCES
Water Highways

Oil is the main cargo passing through Gulf waters. Most is shipped to Europe, the United States, Canada, and Japan. A large amount of oil traffic passes through the Red Sea as well because ships travel this way to reach the Suez Canal. A variety of goods comes south through the canal—some of the biggest shipments are cereals from North America, fertilizers, and machinery. The cargoes are not just for Middle Eastern countries, but also for Asian and even Australian ports far beyond.

The majority of ships are tankers, and the largest, called supertankers, can carry about 500,000 tons of oil and are over 1,300 ft. long. Navigating these ships can be difficult.

An oil tanker docks at a special pier built out into the sea in Kuwait. Pipes feed oil directly into the tanks in the holds of the ship.

A cargo ship sails through the Suez Canal. The canal has been built through the desert to link the Mediterranean Sea with the Red Sea.

In the Red Sea the narrow channels are restricted by coral, and in the Gulf there is a lot of other traffic to avoid. The straits at the southern ends of both seas are narrow and shallow, and ships have to be guided through carefully.

The Suez Canal is an important shortcut for international sea transportation because it avoids the need for ships to take the long route around Africa. Without the canal, an empty tanker returning from northwest Europe to Saudi Arabia would take 36 days sailing round Africa, but it can do the journey in 22 days via the canal. The canal is basically a deep trench cut through the narrow neck of land between the Mediterranean and Red Sea. Sections of the canal pass through shallow lakes in which channels have been dredged.

Although oil traffic is still a large share of Suez Canal business, Middle Eastern oil exporters use the canal less than they once did. The Six-Day War in 1967 closed the canal, and producers found other ways of transporting oil. Supertankers were developed to carry oil cheaply in bulk, and oil pipelines were built. Even though the canal is now open again and has been deepened and widened, many supertankers are too big to use the canal when they are fully loaded. Pipelines such as the Sumed Pipeline, which is already carrying twice the amount of oil passing through canal, are likely to take more oil in the future.

The Suez Canal	
Opened	1869
Length	100 mi.
Width	Varies, but some sections are not wide enough for two ships to pass through.
Depth	55 ft.
Average travel time	15 hours
Red Sea Terminus	Suez
Mediterranean Terminus	Port Said

USES AND RESOURCES
Harvest of the Seas

Fish are an important part of the diet for people who live along desert coasts. Many kinds of fish are caught in the Red Sea and Gulf, from little fish, such as sardines and snappers, to larger sharks and barracudas. The seagrass beds in the shallow waters of the Gulf are particularly rich in shrimps.

Yemeni fishermen bring in their catch on the beach. There is a rich variety of fish in both the Red Sea and the Gulf of Aden, and Yemen has a growing fishing industry.

Some fishermen still use their traditional boats to catch small amounts of fish for food or for sale at local markets. There is more small-scale traditional fishing in the Red Sea than in the Gulf. People in the Gulf have become less dependent on fishing for their livelihoods since the discovery of oil, and fishing has become **commercialized**. Fleets of motor trawlers bring fish and shrimps into ports at Bahrain, Kuwait, and Qatar. Because of the heat, most ships are refrigerated to keep the fish fresh until it is brought to shore.

Fish stocks are falling in the northern part of the Arabian Gulf because dams on the Tigris and Euphrates rivers are stopping nutrients, upon which so much sea life depends, from entering the sea. Pollution of the water from oil spills is also taking its toll on fish catches, particularly the important shrimp industry.

One of the oldest industries in the Gulf is pearl fishing. Pearls are found in oysters and are worn as jewelery. For hundreds of years, good quality pearls were harvested from oysters in sandy, shallow bays in the Gulf. Bahrain was one of the main pearling centers. At one time as many as 40,000 people from all over the Arabian Peninsula were employed in pearling. Divers would swim underwater for minutes at a time, holding their breath while they filled baskets with oysters. During the 1930s, the Japanese found a way of farming oysters to produce pearls, known as cultured pearls, which were much easier to harvest. The oil business also attracted people away from pearling in the Gulf, and as a result pearling has now almost died out in the region.

An Egyptian fish seller. A lot of the fishing in the Red Sea is still just for local markets and done on a small scale in a traditional way.

Old Resources, New Resources

Before the discovery of oil, salt was one of the most valuable minerals found in the Gulf. In the past, salt was used to help preserve food, and it still is an essential part of a person's diet. Along the shallow Arabian coasts of the Gulf, there are large areas of natural salt flats, called *sebkhas*, where the hot sun has evaporated the seawater. Mixed with mud and sand, the salt lies as a thick crust up to 3 ft. thick. For hundreds of years, blocks of salt were dug up and taken by camel inland to market. Although the salt industry is now less important, salt is still extracted from the *sebkhas*.

Relatively little oil has been found in the Red Sea, but scientists have discovered another mineral resource that might be used in the future. Below the hot, salty water in the

One of the largest Red Sea holiday resorts is at Eilat, in Israel, in the Gulf of Aqaba.

A diver watches a grouper fish. The clear waters and wonderful sea life make the Red Sea one of the most popular places in the world for diving.

deep clefts of the Red Sea is a thick, muddy sediment containing large quantities of valuable metals such as iron, zinc, and copper. The minerals lie so deep that no one has yet found an easy way to extract them, but it may be possible to pump up the muddy sediment to a ship and then extract the minerals.

It is only in recent years that tourists have started to appreciate the lovely coral reefs and the clear, warm waters of the Red Sea. The fantastic variety of sea life is a spectacular sight. Many tourists, especially divers, visit the Red Sea every year, but there are still relatively few resorts, and they are mostly along the Egyptian coast. The beauty and interest of the reefs could attract more tourists and money to the poorer countries in the area, such as Sudan, but careful control is needed to preserve the reefs and their wildlife. There are fears that too many tourists would disturb fish and that pollution from big tourist developments might kill coral and other sea creatures. Egypt has already set up marine conservation areas, where diving is controlled.

THE FUTURE
Rich Seas, Troubled Seas

The discovery of oil has brought greater changes to the region than anything else in the last few hundred years. Some countries have become fabulously wealthy—Saudi Arabia and Kuwait are now two of the richest countries in the world. The money has enabled them to build houses, factories, and roads and provide good welfare services such as schools and hospitals for their people. They can also afford to provide fresh water, both for cities and new farms in the desert, using the expensive desalination process.

Other Muslim countries around the Arabian Gulf have benefited as well. Thousands of people have jobs working in the oil business, and the richer states have helped poorer Muslim neighbors by giving them money for new projects.

Even though the oil has brought wealth, it has also brought trouble. There have been several disputes over ownership of the oil-rich territories, such as Iraq's invasion of Kuwait in 1990. The invasion became a major world incident because of international worries about protecting future oil supplies. Thousands of people were killed in the fighting, and there

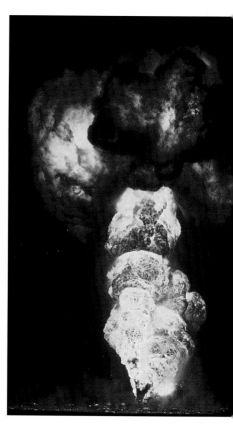

Above: An oil well burns in Kuwait at the end of the Gulf War, belching black smoke and blotting out the sun. It was several months before all the fires were put out.

Oil has brought great wealth to countries such as Saudi Arabia, which have been able to build modern hospitals such as this one for their people.

was massive oil pollution in the Arabian Gulf when oil wells were destroyed or set on fire. Clouds of black smoke filled the air, and oil leaked out across land and water, contaminating desalination plants and poisoning wildlife in the sea.

The vast amounts of oil being extracted and transported around the Red Sea and Arabian Gulf pose great dangers to the environment of the seas. The risks are greater than in an open ocean because the seas are virtually enclosed, and it could take a long time for pollution to be washed away (although the warm water and sunshine in the area are a help in breaking down oil pollution). Oil spills occur regularly despite controls over safety on oil tankers, rigs, and pipelines. However, there is concern for the environment in this area, and regional action plans have been set up to watch over the two seas. There is hope that pollution can be controlled so that the rich, varied natural life in the Red Sea and Arabian Gulf will not be harmed.

Despite the huge amount of shipping traffic that passes through the waters of the Red Sea and Arabian Gulf, these seas remain some of the cleanest and most unspoiled in the world.

Glossary

algae Simple water plants, ranging in size from microscopic phytoplankton to giant seaweed.

aquifers Rocks that contain water within their pores or joints. They form underground reservoirs of water that can be reached by wells.

barrier reefs Coral reefs found farther out at sea in deeper water. They are usually separated from the shore by wide lagoons.

colonize To conquer, settle in, and control another country.

commercialized Used to make a profit.

continent A large area of land, for example, Africa.

decomposing Decaying.

delta A flat, fan-shaped area of land where the mouth of a river approaches the sea.

desalinate A process by which salt is removed from seawater so that it can be used as fresh water.

dredged When a canal, river, or other waterway is deepened.

evaporates When a liquid, such as water, heats up and changes into a vapor.

forage To search for food to eat.

fringing reefs Coral reefs lying close to the shore.

geological history The history of how the earth and its rocks have developed.

habitat A particular type of place where plants and creatures live.

irrigation Using channels or pipes to water the land.

isthmus A narrow piece of land connecting two larger pieces of land.

lagoons Areas of seawater, rather like lakes, separated from the open sea by sandbanks or reefs.

landlocked Completely, or almost completely, surrounded by land.

navigate To find a safe route for a ship.

nomadic A type of lifestyle that involves moving from place to place to find food and water.

nutrients Basic substances such as minerals that are dissolved in water.

oases Fertile patches in deserts.

oil reserves Underground reservoirs of oil that have not yet been tapped or exploited.

organic Describes something that comes from an animal or plant. Organic sediments are small particles made up of the dead remains of plants and creatures.

peninsula An area of land mainly surrounded by sea but joined to a larger area of land.

pilgrimage A journey to a holy place.

predators Animals that hunt and kill other creatures for food.

refined Processed to get rid of impurities.

scrub Bushes and small trees.

seasonal Something that happens only at certain times, or seasons, of the year.

sediment Fine particles of rock and earth, such as mud and sand.

silt Very fine mud or clay that is carried along by a river.

squalls Sudden, strong winds or brief, violent storms.

strait A narrow sea channel that has formed between two areas of land.

subsistence Making a living that provides only the basic necessities, such as food and water, of life.

tankers Large ships that can carry liquid cargo.

tidal range The difference between the height of the water at low and high tide.

treaties Formal agreements between countries.

Further Information

There are very few books about the Red Sea and Arabian Gulf, so look out for general books about seas and oceans and countries of the Middle East.

FURTHER READING:

Department of Geography, ed. *Iran in Pictures*. Visual Geography. Minneapolis, MN: Lerner Group, 1992.

————. *Iraq in Pictures*. Visual Geography. Minneapolis, MN: Lerner Group, 1992.

Ganeri, Anita. *The Oceans Atlas*. New York: Dorling Kindersley, 1994.

Gibbs, B. *Ocean Facts*. Facts and Lists. Tulsa, OK: Educational Development Corp., 1991.

Honeyman, Susannah. *Saudi Arabia*. Country Fact Files. Austin, TX: Raintree Steck-Vaughn, 1995.

Janin, Hunt. *Saudi Arabia*. Tarrytown, NY: Marshall Cavendish, 1992.

Pateman, Robert. *Egypt*. Cultures of the World. Tarrytown, NY: Marshall Cavendish, 1992.

CD ROMS:

Geopedia: The Multimedia Geography CD-Rom. Chicago: Encyclopedia Britannica.

Habitats. Austin, TX: Raintree Steck-Vaughn, 1996.

USEFUL ADDRESSES:

Center for Environmental Education, Center for Marine Conservation, 1725 De Sales Street NW, Suite 500, Washington, DC 20036

Earthwatch Headquarters, 680 Mount Auburn Street, P.O. Box 403, Watertown, MA 02272-9104

Index